Famous Myths and Legends of the World

Myths and Legends of
SCANDINAVIA

WORLD
BOOK

a Scott Fetzer company
Chicago
www.worldbook.com

World Book, Inc.
180 North LaSalle Street
Suite 900
Chicago, Illinois 60601
USA

For information about other World Book publications, visit our website at **www.worldbook.com** or call **1-800-967-5325.**

Library of Congress Cataloging-in-Publication Data

Myths and legends of Scandinavia.
    pages cm. -- (Famous myths and legends of the world)
    Summary: "Myths and legends from Scandinavia. Features include information about the history and culture behind the myths, pronunciations, lists of deities, word glossary, further information, and index"-- Provided by publisher.
    Includes index.
    ISBN 978-0-7166-2636-7
    1. Mythology, Norse--Juvenile literature. 2. Gods, Norse--Juvenile literature. 3. Scandinavia--Folklore--Juvenile literature. I. World Book, Inc. II. Series: Famous myths and legends of the world.
    BL863.M98 2015
    398.20948--dc23
                        2015014767

Set ISBN: 978-0-7166-2625-1
E-book ISBN: 978-0-7166-2648-0 (EPUB3)

Printed in China by PrintWORKS Global Services, Shenzhen, Guangdong
2nd printing May 2016

Writer: Scott A. Leonard

Staff for World Book, Inc.
Executive Committee
President: Jim O'Rourke
Vice President and Editor in Chief: Paul A. Kobasa
Vice President, Finance: Donald D. Keller
Vice President, Marketing: Jean Lin
Director, International Sales: Kristin Norell
Director, Human Resources: Bev Ecker

Digital
Director of Digital Products Development: Erika Meller
Digital Products Coordinator: Matthew Werner

Editorial
Manager, Annuals/Series Nonfiction: Christine Sullivan
Managing Editor, Annuals/Series Nonfiction:
    Barbara Mayes
Administrative Assistant: Ethel Matthews
Manager, Indexing Services: David Pofelski
Manager, Contracts & Compliance
    (Rights & Permissions): Loranne K. Shields

Manufacturing/Production
Manufacturing Manager: Sandra Johnson
Production/Technology Manager: Anne Fritzinger
Proofreader: Nathalie Strassheim

Graphics and Design
Senior Art Director: Tom Evans
Coordinator, Design Development and Production:
    Brenda Tropinski
Senior Designers: Matthew Carrington,
    Isaiah W. Sheppard, Jr.
Media Researcher: Rosalia Calderone
Manager, Cartographic Services: Wayne K. Pichler
Senior Cartographer: John M. Rejba

Staff for Brown Bear Books Ltd
Managing Editor: Tim Cooke
Editorial Director: Lindsey Lowe
Children's Publisher: Anne O'Daly
Design Manager: Keith Davis
Designer: Mike Davis
Picture Manager: Sophie Mortimer

Picture credits
t=top, c=center, b=bottom, l=left, r=right
4bl, Thinkstock; 5t, Thinkstock; 6, Topfoto; 7, WORLD BOOK map; 8-9, Thinkstock; 10-11l, Shutterstock; 12b, Shutterstock; 12-13t, Shutterstock; 13tr, Thinkstock; 13b, Topfoto; 14-15, Shutterstock; 16-17, Topfoto; 18, Alamy; 18-19t, Shutterstock; 18-19b, The Kobal Collection; 19br, Topfoto; 21, Topfoto; 23, Topfoto; 24b, Thinkstock; 24-25t, Topfoto; 25bl, Thinkstock; 25br, Alamy; 26-27, Alamy; 28-29b, Alamy; 28-29, Shutterstock; 30, Alamy; 30-31t, Topfoto; 31b, Alamy; 33-35t, Topfoto; 35b, Getty Images; 37-39, Arthur Rackham; 40, Arthur Rackham; 40-41, Alamy; 43, Arthur Rackham; 45, Arthur Rackham; 46, Arthur Rackham; 47t, Alamy; 47bl, Topfoto; 48-49, Shutterstock; 50-51, Dreamstime; 52-53t, Topfoto; 53t, Dreamstime; 53b Topfoto; 54-55, Thinkstock; 56-57, Dreamstime; 58bl, Alamy; 59tr, RHL; 59bl, Thinkstock; 59br, Dreamstime, back cover, Shutterstock.

CONTENTS

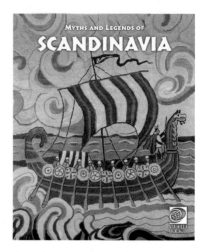

The Viking explorer Leif Eriksson leads his men to North America. Leif was the son of Erik the Red, who established the first European settlement in what is now Greenland.

The Coming of the Norsemen in 1000 AD (circa 1960), tapestry by Mabelle Linnea Holmes; Jamestown-Yorktown Educational Trust, Williamsburg, VA (Bridgeman Images)

Note to Readers:

Phonetic pronunciations have been inserted into the myths and legends in this volume to make reading the stories easier and to give the reader some of the flavor of the cultures of Scandinavia the stories represent. See page 64 for a pronunciation key.

The myths and legends retold in this volume are written in a creative way to provide an engaging reading experience and approximate the artistry of the originals. Many of these stories were not written down but were recited by storytellers from generation to generation. Even when some of the stories came to be written down they likely did not feature phonetic pronunciations for challenging names and words! We hope the inclusion of this material will improve rather than distract from your experience of the stories.

Some of the figures mentioned in the myths and legends in this volume are described on page 60 in the section "Deities of Scandinavia." In addition, some unusual words in the text are defined in the Glossary on page 62.

INTRODUCTION

Since the earliest times, people have told stories to try to explain the world in which they lived. These stories are known as myths. Myths try to answer these kinds of questions: How was the world created? Who were the first people? Where did animals come from? Why does the sun rise and set? Why is the land devastated by storms or drought? Today, people often rely on science to answer many of these questions. But in earlier times—and in some parts of the world today—people have explained natural events using stories about gods, goddesses, nature spirits, and heroes.

Myths are different from folk tales and legends. Folk tales are fictional stories about animals or human beings. Most of these tales are not set in any particular time or place, and they begin and end in a certain way. For example, many English folk tales begin with the phrase "Once upon a time" and end with "They lived happily ever after." Legends are set in the real world, in the present or the historical past. Legends distort the truth, but they are based on real people or events.

The World of Fenrir, page 24

Myths, in contrast, typically tell of events that have taken place in the remote past. Unlike legends, myths have also played—and often continue to play—an important role in a society's religious life. Although legends may have religious themes, most are not religious in nature. The people of a society may tell folk tales and legends for amusement, without believing them. But they usually consider their myths sacred and completely true.

Most myths concern *divinities* or *deities* (divine beings). These divinities have powers far greater than those of any human being. At the same time, however, many gods, goddesses, and heroes of mythology have human characteristics. They are guided by such emotions as love and jealousy, and they may experience birth and death. Mythological figures may even look like human beings. Often, the human qualities of the divinities reflect a society's ideals. Good gods and goddesses have the qualities a society admires, and evil ones have the qualities it dislikes. In myths, the actions of these divinities influence the world of humans for better or for worse.

Myths may seem very strange. They sometimes seem to take place in a world that is both like our world and unlike it. Time can go backward and forward, so it is sometimes difficult to tell in what order events happen. People may be dead and alive at the same time.

Myths were originally passed down from generation to generation by word of mouth. Partly for this reason, there are often different versions of the same story. Many myths across cultures share similar themes, such as a battle between good and evil. But the myths of a society generally reflect the landscape, climate, and society in which the storytellers lived.

Myths tell people about their distant history. They show people how to behave and find their way. As teaching tools, myths help to prepare children for adulthood.

The World of the Creation, page 12

Myths and Legends of Scandinavia

The myths and legends of northern Europe remain some of the most popular of all ancient stories. They continue to inspire musicians, artists, and writers as well as makers of movies and video games. The myths of northern Europe are often known as Scandinavian mythology. Although Scandinavia is made up of only Denmark, Norway, and Sweden, tales from Finland and Iceland are usually included in this grouping. This mythology is also known as Norse mythology, after the Norse people who lived in Scandinavia during the Middle Ages, or Teutonic mythology, for the Germanic peoples of northern Europe.

The World of Loki, page 34

The basic sources for Scandinavian mythology are the Eddas, two collections of oral, or spoken, poems written down in Iceland in the 1200's. Other information on Scandinavian mythology comes from legends about specific families and heroes and from German literary and historical works.

Scandinavian mythology includes many heroes. Sigurd the Dragon Slayer probably ranks as the most important. He appears in a Scandinavian version of German myths about a royal family called the Volsungs. Sigurd became the model for the mythical German hero Siegfried, who appears in the *Nibelungenlied*, a famous German epic of the Middle Ages.

Scandinavian mythology is unique among the mythologies of other western cultures because it includes an *eschatology* (account of the end of the world). Scandinavian mythology predicts that one day, there will be a great battle called Ragnarok. This battle will be fought between the giants, led by Loki, the trickster god, and the gods and goddesses who live in a world called Asgard. All of these beings will die in the battle, and Earth will be destroyed by fire. After the battle, Balder, the god of beauty and goodness, will be reborn and form a new race of divinities. The human race will also be re-created. The new world, cleansed of evil and treachery, will endure forever.

Although many of the stories in this book appear simple at first glance, they are layered with meaning. Retellings of the stories often reveal new insights. By studying myths, we can learn how different societies have answered basic questions about the world and the individual's place in it. We can better understand the feelings and values that bind members of society into one group. By comparing the myths of various cultures, we can discover how these cultures differ and how they resemble one another. And myths can help us understand why people behave as they do.

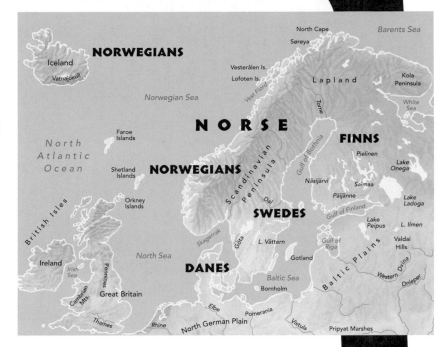

Scandinavian mythology, also known as Norse or Teutonic mythology, includes stories from Scandinavia (Denmark, Norway, and Sweden), Iceland, Finland, and Germany.

The CREATION
and Peopling of the World

After the universe began in fire and ice, Odin and his brothers killed their grandfather, Ymir, to create the world. They created Ask and Embla, the first humans, and shaped the universe.

It all began in silence and darkness, in heat and cold. Muspelheim (MOO spell haym), the fire-world, emerged before all else, shining bright in the silent darkness. Soon, foggy Niflheim (NIHV uhl haym), the ice-world, appeared, glinting like starlight on frost.

Fire from Muspelheim and ice from Niflheim met in a great emptiness that lay between them, forming the waters. Out of the waters, the frost giant Ymir (EE mihr) was born, the first living thing. Ymir grew rapidly on the milk from the first cow. As Ymir grew, he gave birth to three beings. They came from his armpits and from one leg. And so a divine race of giants was born.

The first cow then licked a huge block of salt, eventually revealing another giant named Buri (BOO ree). Buri created a son, whom he named Bor (bawr). In time, Bor married the Giantess Bestla (BEHST lah), one of Ymir's daughters. And soon, Bestla gave birth to three sons, Odin (OH dihn), Vili (VIHL ee), and Vé (vay), who founded the first race of gods.

When he grew to become a man, war-hungry Odin, All-Father of the Gods, led his brothers against Ymir. Together the brothers slew the giant, who was their grandfather.

From Ymir's body, the brothers fashioned the world. Ymir's blood became the seas. His bones became the rugged mountains. The hairs on Ymir's head became the trees. Ymir's skull formed the sky's dome above us. Finally, the sons of Bor used Ymir's eyebrows to create Midgard (MIHD gahrd), a home for humans.

In Ymir's flesh, maggots appeared. Odin, the All-Father, granted the maggots a human appearance and intelligence, but these creatures continued to live in mountains and caves. These were the Dwarves. Their world is known as Nidavellir (nihth ah vehl ihr). Odin also gave life to the Elves. They dwell in fair Alfheim (AHLF haym), a peaceful kingdom.

Odin married Frigg (frihg), the goddess of love and marriage. From them descended the Aesir (EYE seer) and the Vanir (VAH nihr), the twin tribes of valiant gods of Earth, water, air, sky, and all other things.

Once while walking along the shores of the sea, Odin, Vili, and Vé came upon two trees, an ash and an elm. From the ash tree, they formed a man; from the elm, they fashioned a woman.

Odin gave the first human couple spirit and life. Vili gave them motion and rationality. And Vé provided them with clothing and names. The man was called Ask and the woman was called Embla (EHM blah). They were the ancestors of all the people who live or have lived in Midgard. And so Odin, the All-Father, gave life and being to humans and gods.

Odin and his children built Asgard (AS gahrd)—the Upper World—as a home for the gods. When mighty Odin took the high seat in his mead hall, he saw past, present, and future. All lives and actions in all the Nine Worlds of the Universe were visible to the All-Father. Odin and his children also built the Bifrost (BEE fruhst), the Rainbow Bridge connecting Asgard and Midgard, so the gods could come to and go from our world as they pleased.

But not all beings in the Nine Worlds were the children of Odin. The Norns came forth from the silence and darkness that existed before the appearance of Muspelheim, the fire-world, and Niflheim, the ice-world. The Norns looked like women at different stages of life. Urd, a shriveled crone, was That Which Has Been. Verdandi (ver dahn dee), a beautiful woman in her prime, was That Which Takes Shape Now. Skuld (skoold), a sweet-faced girl, was the Shaper of Things Yet to Come. These three beings wove and unwove the threads that determined the fate of gods and people.

The Norns lived by the roots of Yggdrasil (IHG drah sihl), the Universal Ash Tree, which supported creation. The Nine Worlds of the Universe, including Midgard, Asgard, and all other worlds of the Universe hung in its branches. Yggdrasil's roots drew life from the Well of Urd, which contained the energies of all things that have happened and continue to happen. Sitting on his mighty eight-legged horse, Sleipnir (SLAYP nihr), Odin rode as he wished up and down the trunk of the mighty tree, visiting the worlds and gaining wisdom. He sometimes walked disguised as a mortal in the world of humans.

The World of
THE CREATION

The Norse were the early inhabitants of modern-day Denmark, Finland, Iceland, Norway, and Sweden. The most famous group of Norse are known to us today as the Vikings. Their ancestors were Germanic peoples who once lived in northwestern Europe. Beginning about 2000 B.C., these peoples moved to what is now Scandinavia (Denmark, Norway, and Sweden). Separate groups of Vikings developed in each of these areas, though the three groups shared the same general culture. The Vikings were skilled seafarers and fierce warriors who traded and raided throughout Europe. They also settled in Britain, France, Greenland, Iceland (right), and Russia. Vikings became the first Europeans to reach North America.

A reconstruction of a longhouse typical of those found in circular Viking fortresses called *trelleborgs* stands at one such site excavated by archaeologists near Slagelse, Denmark. This fortress, one of seven known trelleborgs, dates from A.D. 980. At least 500 Vikings lived there in 16 houses arranged in four squares. A wide wooden wall and a moat surrounded and protected the fortress.

MEAD

Mead halls were large, one-room buildings that were used by Viking rulers for feasts. The halls were named for the alcoholic drink commonly served there. Mead is prepared by boiling honeycombs in water and *fermenting* (chemically changing) the resulting liquor with yeast. Valhalla (val HAL uh), Odin's mead hall, was said to have walls of gold and a roof made of battle shields. Huge spears held up its ceiling. The shields were so highly polished that the gleam from them was the only light needed. The hall had 540 doors, which were so wide that 800 men could enter side by side. Guests sat at long tables.

Horns, generally from cattle, decorated with silver often served as drinking vessels for the Vikings.

Odin (OH dihn) was the chief god in Norse mythology. Also known as Woden (WOH duhn), he was one of the most complex and mysterious figures in all of mythology. He was both the god of war and the god of poetry. Odin gave up one eye for the right to drink from the spring of wisdom, but he cared little for such social values as community, justice, and respect for the law.

Odin was also known for his magic powers. By wounding and hanging himself from a tree, he acquired the power of casting spells called *runes*. These spells let Odin predict the future, change his shape, and visit the underworld. According to Norse myths, Odin would lead the gods against the evil giants at Ragnarok (RAHG nuh ROK), the battle that would destroy the world.

13

THE WAR BETWEEN THE
AESIR AND THE VANIR

When Odin and the other Aesir tried to kill Gullveig—in reality the Vanir goddess Freyja—the two tribes of Norse gods went to war. Even when peace returned, the tribes remained quarrelsome.

The Aesir (EYE seer) and the Vanir (VAH nihr) were twin tribes of gods whose kingdoms—Asgard (AS gahrd) and Vanaheim (VAN uh haym)—lay near each other in the uppermost branches of Yggdrasil (IHG drah sihl), the Universal Tree. In ancient times, Freyja (FRAY uh), the Vanir goddess of beauty, fertility, and magic, came to Asgard in the form of Gullveig (GAHL vayg). She had great *seidr* (say duhr), the power to find hidden things and change the course of events. The Aesir sought her for her gifts, particularly her ability to bring gold to those seeking her favor.

All-Father Odin (OH dihn) perceived that the love of gold was corrupting the Aesir. He decided he needed to restore his children's honor. When word of Odin's decision reached the Aesir, they appointed Gullveig as their representative. Seated in Odin's mead hall, Gullveig told the All-Father that any threat against the Aesir would bring war. As a show of force, she demonstrated her powerful seidr. Outraged that Gullveig would defy him so openly in his own hall, Odin broke his rule against shedding blood in his hall and cast his spear into Gullveig.

Shamed by Odin, the Aesir blamed Gullveig for their greed and likewise threw their spears into her body. They then flung her body on the fire. But Gullveig emerged from the ashes unharmed. Again the Aesir cast their spears into her and burned her body. And again Gullweig emerged unharmed. This happened a third time with the same result.

News of this outrage soon reached the ears of the Vanir, particularly of Njord (nyoord), the god of the sea and the

wind. Njord's fury was kindled. Soon, the armored Vanir brought war to Asgard. "Revenge for our Queen of Seidr!" they cried as they stormed the gates.

Looking out on the Vanir, Odin was surprised at how few of them there seemed to be and how disorganized they appeared. The Aesir, accustomed to face-to-face combat and the use of swords, battle-axes, and shields, rushed from the gates. They expected to destroy such a small number of enemies with a quick strike.

But the Aesir were deceived. The Vanir's powerful magic rendered many of their warriors invisible. And instead of the usual weapons, the Vanir used magical weapons, including the sword of Freyja's brother Freyr (frayr), which devastated his enemies, without his having to wield it. To the disgust of Odin, victory in that first skirmish went to the Vanir. But valiant Thor (thawr), the Aesir god of lightning and thunder, fought back. Soon the Aesir and the Vanir had each counted up glorious victories and terrible losses. But neither side gained an advantage.

Brooding in their separate camps, Odin and Njord mourned how few warriors they had left. Soon their peoples would

vanish, unless a way to peace could be found. But peace is a tricky business. Blood that is spilled demands just compensation. One must either get revenge for the fallen or extract a price for the deaths from one's enemies.

Finally, a truce was declared. Both sides paid the blood-price in treasure to honor their enemy's valiant dead. The two groups also agreed to exchange hostages

to serve as a living tribute to those who had lost their lives. The Vanir sent Njord and his children, Freyja and Freyr, to live in Asgard. The Aesir sent Hoenir (HOO nihr) and Mimir (MEE mihr), the wisest of gods, to live in Vanaheim. The Vanir hostages lived peacefully among the Aesir. But the Vanir grew unhappy with their hostage Hoenir. At times, he seemed capable of great wisdom. At other times he seemed confused and would say "I have no advice to give you." What the Vanir failed to notice was that Hoenir was capable of wisdom only when Mimir was present to advise him.

Feeling cheated, the Vanir beheaded Mimir and sent his head to Odin. Odin was horrified. But by using magic and herbs, Odin preserved Mimir's head, which provided him with excellent counsel ever after.

The World of
THE **AESIR** AND THE **VANIR**

Religion, which included magic, was important to the Vikings, who worshiped many gods. For the Vikings, *seidr* (say duhr) was a form of magic concerned chiefly with understanding and changing the course of destiny. The Vikings saw destiny as woven of many threads that could be rewoven to reshape the course of events. Those skilled in seidr attempted to reveal hidden patterns so the threads leading to a possible outcome could be altered. But seidr was also used for cursing individuals and actions. Contact between the Vikings and European Christians led to the end of the Viking religion. English and German missionaries helped make Christianity the chief religion in Scandinavia by the early 1100's.

TO GO A-VIKING

The Vikings did not call themselves by that name. The name *Viking* did not come into use until after the Viking Age, which lasted from the late A.D. 700's to about 1100. The name probably came from Vik, a pirate center in southern Norway during Viking times. Among the Scandinavians, the expression *to go a-viking* meant *to fight as a pirate or warrior*. Other Europeans called the Scandinavians *Norsemen, Northmen,* or *Danes.*

Viking myths are popular in the modern world. British author J. R. R. Tolkien drew on Norse myths as he wrote *The Hobbit* (1937) and *The Lord of the Rings* (1954–1955). One of the names given to Odin is "the Grey Pilgrim," a stranger who wanders the world in a grey cloak and cap. This figure was an inspiration for Tolkien's wizard Gandalf the Gray.

The Vikings believed the Norn goddesses (left) wove and unwove the threads of fate. They looked like three women at different stages of their lives.

Lush turf shelters buildings at a reconstructed Viking farm in Iceland. (Turf is soil covered with grasses and other small plants.) Few Scandinavians of the Viking Age spent their time going a-viking. Most worked as farmers or in other peaceful occupations.

Viking warriors were bold and enjoyed fighting. They were also brutal and fearsome. They fought with swords, battle-axes, and round wooden shields and wore helmets made of iron. During their raids, they killed women and children as well as men. Often, what they did not steal, they burned. The Vikings so terrorized other Europeans that one French church created a special prayer for protection: "God, deliver us from the fury of the Northmen."

THE BINDING OF FENRIR

The children of the trickster god Loki and the giantess Angrboda were all enemies of the gods of Asgard, but the most terrifying of the three was the hideous wolf Fenrir.

The Aesir (EYE seer) had no love for Loki (LOH kee), the Trickster. He could be trusted only to please himself. How else to explain that he mixed with the enemy—the Giants—and had children by the giantess Angrboda (AHNG guhr boh duh)? And what monsters these children were! All-Father Odin (OH dihn), from his high seat, foresaw that the children of Loki would bring disaster not only to the Aesir but also the inhabitants of the other eight worlds that made up the Universe.

So the Aesir tried to confine the children of Loki and Angrboda. The firstborn was Jormungandr (YAWR muhn guhn dahr), a serpent that was fated to kill

Thor (thawr) during Ragnarok (RAHG nuh ROK), the battle that ends all days. The Aesir threw Jormungandr into the ocean that surrounded Midgard (MIHD gahrd), where the serpent grew quickly. Soon it encircled Midgard and was able to put its own tail in its mouth! Loki and Angrboda's second child was greedy, hideous Hel. She was banished to Helheim (HEL haym), sometimes called Niflheim (NIHV uhl haym), the dark world of ice-fog. Said to be half corpse and half living woman, Hel prevented the souls of those who die of old age, accident, and disease from returning to the light.

But the wolf Fenrir (fehn rihr) was the most fearsome of Loki and Angrboda's

children. Fenrir terrified the Aesir. Only Tyr (tihr), dispenser of justice in battle, was bold enough to approach and feed the wolf pup.

And that pup grew at astonishing speed! The Aesir could not stand having the beast in Asgard (AS gahrd). But neither could they let it run free. So they attempted to bind the monster wolf with chains. They gained Fenrir's consent for this by telling him that the chains were tests of his strength. As Fenrir burst each of his ever-stronger bindings, the Aesir cheered him, though they found it amazing and frightening.

Growing desperate, the Aesir sent a messenger to Nidavellir (nihth ah VEHL ihr) to enlist the Dwarves' help. Through expert craft and magic, the Dwarves combined a cat's footsteps, a woman's beard, the roots of a mountain, the breath of a fish, and the spit of a bird to fashion the Gleipnir (GLAYP nihr), a binding whose name means *the open one.*

At first, Fenrir smelled magic on the strange new binding and grew suspicious. He refused to allow anyone to place Gleipnir on him. "Only if someone places his or her hand in my jaws as a pledge of trust," growled the monster wolf, "will I consent to try my strength against this Gleipnir."

Tyr, realizing that a sacrifice was needed for the good of all, boldly approached Fenrir and laid his hand in the wolf's mouth. Then the Aesir bound Fenrir with Gleipnir. The monster wolf struggled and struggled but could not break free.

When Fenrir realized he could not escape the new binding, he bit down on Tyr's hand and swallowed it whole. But Fenrir was still trapped. The Aesir transported Fenrir to a lonely mountain, placing a sword in his jaws so he could not bite anyone else. To this day, Fenrir remains chained and muzzled on the mountain, waiting for Ragnarok, when Gleipnir will fail and Fenrir will get revenge by devouring Odin, the All-Father.

23

The World of FENRIR

The Vikings believed that the world would end in a totally destructive battle called Ragnarok (RAHG nuh ROK), or the Twilight of the Gods (right). The battle was to be fought between the Giants, led by Loki (LOH kee), and the gods and goddesses living in Asgard (AS gahrd). Fenrir (fehn rihr) the wolf (red in illustration) would kill Odin (OH dihn). All the other gods, goddesses, and giants would also be killed. A series of natural disasters would then strike Earth, and a final, huge flood would sweep away all life from the surface of the planet. After the battle, Balder (BAWL duhr), the god of light and beauty, would be reborn. With several sons of dead gods, he would form a new race of divinities. The human race would also be re-created. The new world, cleansed of evil and treachery, would endure forever.

Dwarves were common characters in northern European myths. They had a human form and were said to live deep within Earth. They were often shown as little men with long beards (left). Dwarves had supernatural origins, but they were not gods themselves. Dwarves were often associated with great skill in magic and in metalworking. This ability was important to peoples whose smiths made iron swords and spear tips for warriors and iron tools for farmers.

GIANTS

Giants appear in every country's mythology. The Norse giants lived in Jotunheim (YAW tun haym), on the northwestern edge of Earth. It is one of the Nine Worlds of the Universe on Yggdrasil (IHG drah sihl), the Universal Ash Tree. The ancient Greeks and Romans believed people had grown smaller as time passed. They thought their ancestors had been huge individuals of great strength and power. Welsh giants are well known through the story of Jack the Giant Killer. One of the most famous giants in literature is Goliath (guh LY uhth), who is described in the Hebrew Bible as 10 feet (300 centimeters) tall.

The Giantess Angrboda (AHNG guhr boh duh) (far left) sits with her three monstrous children who were fathered by Loki (LOH kee), the Trickster god. They were Jormungandr (YAWR muhn guhn dahr), the serpent; Fenrir (fehn rihr), the wolf; and Hel, said to be half living woman and half corpse, who became queen of the underworld.

THE DEATH OF BALDER

The gods were heartbroken to learn that Odin's son Balder would soon die. When Balder's mother, Frigg, gained promises from all living things not to harm her son—apart from one—Loki saw a chance for mischief.

Joyful Balder (BAWL duhr), the son of Odin (OH dihn), was loved by all. His courage, generosity, and warmth gladdened all hearts. So when Balder began having dreams predicting that he would die soon, the gloom among the Aesir (EYE seer) was like the first frost at end of summer. "Odin, All-Father," pleaded the Aesir, "do something!"

Odin disguised himself, saddled his eight-legged steed, Sleipnir (SLAYP nihr), and flew down from the Aesir's home in Asgard (AS gahrd) for nine days until he reached the realm of the dead. There he looked for the spirit of a long-dead prophetess who was exceptionally gifted in reading the threads of destiny woven by the three Norns. To Odin's surprise,

the icy and fog-shrouded halls were decorated in preparation for a great feast.

"What is the happy occasion?" Odin asked the spirit of the dead prophetess. Not recognizing the All-Father because of his disguise, the dead woman chatted excitedly about how Balder would soon die and be a guest of honor at the feast they were preparing.

Odin returned to Asgard with a heavy heart and told the Aesir what he had learned. The gods were heartbroken, not only because they loved Balder but also because they knew his death would mark a turning point. With

Balder's passing, the Age of Summer would end for the Nine Worlds of the Universe. Now all worlds would enter the Age of Decline, which would end in utter destruction at Ragnarok (RAHG nuh ROK), the final battle.

But Frigg (frihg), Balder's mother, resisted this destiny. She traveled the world, asking everyone and everything she found to take an oath not to harm Balder. She returned to Asgard, satisfied that her son was now safe.

However, Loki (LOH kee), sensing an opportunity for mischief, transformed himself into an old woman and asked Frigg. "Did you really extract oaths from all to ensure your son's safety?"

"Nearly all," Frigg replied. "Oh?" Loki asked, "Did someone or something refuse to pledge?" "All whom I approached pledged, but I did not bother with mistletoe, which is so small and harmless, it did not seem worth the effort," Frigg foolishly revealed to the disguised Trickster.

The Aesir were happy to learn that Frigg had ensured Balder's safety so they gave a great feast. They made a game of throwing things—stones, knives, and sticks—at Balder, laughing when they bounced harmlessly off the gentle god. Only the blind god Hoder was excluded from the game. Sitting next to him, Loki said, "Why should you miss out on all the fun, Hoder? Let me help you."

Loki put a sprig of mistletoe in the blind god's hand, pointing him in Balder's direction. The tiny branch fluttered through the air, and to everyone's horror, passed right through Balder's heart, striking him dead.

Grief-stricken, the gods refused to accept their loss. "Who will descend to the underworld to negotiate Balder's release?" Odin asked.

One of Odin's sons, Hermod (HER mood), volunteered. Odin put the reins of his horse, Sleipnir, into Hermod's hands, and Hermod made the nine-day journey to Hel's gloomy realm. At last he reached the bridge over the river bordering Helheim.

Modgudr (MUD guh duhr), the grim Giant guarding the bridge, challenged Hermod. "Who are you, stranger?" rumbled the Giant. "Your face appears

as the face of one still living. What is your business with Hel, the Dark Mistress of Helheim (HEL haym)?!"
"I am Hermod, Odin-son, sent by the All-Father to ransom Balder."

Satisfied, Modgudr let Hermod pass. In the mead hall, Hermod found Balder sitting next to Hel. Hermod spoke, "Everyone mourns the death of Balder. The All-Father wishes to ransom my brother. What are your terms?"

"If all throughout the Nine Worlds really mourn," Hel replied, "then let them weep! If all weep, I will return Balder to you. But if even one does not, I keep what is mine."

Messengers were dispatched throughout the Nine Worlds announcing Balder's death. And all wept, except one. Loki assumed the form of the Giant Thokk (thawk) and refused to shed tears. He said to the messengers, "Let Hel keep her own!"

And so Loki ensured that Balder remained in the underworld.

The World of BALDER

The story of Balder (BAWL duhr) had a number of meanings. Balder was a god of fertility, so his death reflected the death of nature in winter. The story was also a reminder that the natural world was full of hidden danger.

THE UNDERWORLD

Myths from around the world tell of gods or heroes like Hermod (HER mood) who travel to the underworld and return. This journey was a symbol of great courage and sacrifice, because it took the traveler into the land of the dead. In Greek myth, the musician Orpheus (AWR fee uhs) descends into Hades (HAY deez) to try to rescue the spirit of his wife, Eurydice (yoo RIHD ih see). The Mayans of Central America told of divine twins who went to the underworld to challenge its rulers to a ball game to rescue their father.

Frigg (frihg) asked all things on Earth to take an oath not to harm her son Balder. Throughout Scandinavia and central Europe, an oath was seen as a sacred promise. It was one of the most important elements in societies in this region. Individuals took an oath to support their rulers or warlords. In return, those rulers took an oath to take care of their subjects. People, especially warriors, went to great lengths to avoid breaking an oath. Some close companions took a special oath to become blood brothers. This oath included a ceremony in which the two companions cut themselves and mixed their blood together.

Much of our knowledge of Norse myth comes from the Eddas (EHD uhs). The term *Edda* refers to two works of medieval Icelandic literature: the *Poetic*, or *Elder*, *Edda* and the *Prose*, or *Younger*, *Edda*. The *Poetic Edda* is a collection of anonymous poems composed in the A.D. 1000's and 1100's. The *Prose Edda* is a textbook for poets written during the 1200's by the Icelandic poet Snorri Sturluson. Snorri's work was the first to be called *Edda*, a name that may be related to an Icelandic word meaning *song* or *poem*.

Norse hunters gallop through the sky at a frenzied pace in an illustration for the *Wild Hunt,* an ancient myth common in Scandinavia and other parts of northern Europe. According to the myth, the appearance of the ghostly huntsmen foretold a coming disaster or the death of witnesses of the apparition. In some versions of the myth, Odin (OH dihn) leads the souls of slain warriors in the hunt.

According to the *Poetic Edda*, Frigg, the goddess of love and marriage, traveled in a chariot drawn by cats given to her by Thor (thawr), the god of the sky.

31

LOKI'S PUNISHMENT

Loki tried to escape punishment for his part in the death of Balder, but it was impossible. When the Aesir caught him, they made sure his punishment fit his terrible crime.

After Loki's (LOH keez) role in the death of Balder (BAWL duhr) was discovered, the Trickster fled to a mountaintop. There he built a stone house with four doors so he might watch for enemies coming from any direction. By day, Loki, the shape-shifter, hid beneath a waterfall in the form of a salmon; by night, he sat by his fire weaving a net to snare fish to eat.

But hiding was useless. From his high seat, Far-Seeing Odin (OH dihn) observed all that passed in the Universe. He knew where Loki was hiding and sent the Aesir (EYE seer) to catch him.

Seeing them coming, Loki threw his net in the fire and cast himself into the stream, again taking on his salmon form. But the Aesir saw the unburned remains of the net in the fire and realized that he must have changed himself into the very prey he hoped to snare in his net. So they rewove the net and began fishing for Loki. In desperation, Loki attempted

to leap over the net and escape. But mighty Thor (thawr) was too quick and grasped him firmly by the tail. This is why the tails of all salmon are so narrow.

Loki was forced to resume his ordinary form. Then the gods made Loki watch as they changed one of his sons into a wolf and killed the other son. In this way, they took double payment for the death of one of Odin's sons. The Giantess Skadi (SKAW dee) used the intestines of Loki's slain son to bind Loki to a rock. Then on a rock above the Trickster's head, she placed a serpent that dripped burning venom on his face.

Loki's faithful wife, Sigyn (SEHG ihn), held a bowl above her husband's head to prevent the venom from burning him. But whenever she went to empty the bowl, the venom spattered Loki's face. His agonized writhing caused earthquakes in Midgard (MIHD gahrd), bringing terror to humankind.

The World of LOKI

The Norse told the story of Loki's (LOH keez) punishment to remind people to cooperate with others in their community, which was vital for survival in the Norse's harsh northern homelands. Loki's punishment may seem harsh, but the death of Balder (BAWL duhr) was only one of many problems he caused for his comrades, the Aesir (EYE seer). In some stories, Loki even causes the death of his companions when it serves his interest.

Another of Loki's victims was Idun (EE duhn) (below), the keeper of the Apples of Eternal Youth, which bestowed immortality on the Aesir. To escape trouble with the Giant Thiazi, Loki helped Thiazi to kidnap Idun. Without the Apples, the gods began to wither with age. Ultimately, the Aesir forced Loki to return Idun to Asgard (AS gahrd).

Loki changed himself into a salmon to try to escape punishment. In another story, he changed himself into a female horse and gave birth to Odin's (OH-dihnz) eight-legged horse, Sleipnir (SLAYP nihr). This ability to change shape was shared by Odin and appears in the myths of many other cultures around the world. The ruler of the Greek gods, Zeus (zoos), transformed himself many times, including into a bull, a swan, and even golden rain.

← Loki's wife, Sigyn (SEHG ihn), holds up a bowl to protect her husband from the burning venom of the snake above him.

A skald (skawld), a Norse poet, recites myths about the gods and heroes to an enthralled audience, in an engraving from the 1800's. The word *skald* is Icelandic for *poet*. From the A.D. 900's through the 1200's, most poets in Norse courts came from Iceland. Most skaldic poetry honored the rulers whom the skalds served. Many of these poems are preserved in the Icelandic *sagas* of the 1100's and 1200's. Skaldic poetry was very complex. It had patterns of *alliteration* (linking words by the repetition of their first sound) and *consonance* (a kind of rhyme between syllables containing different vowels but ending in the same consonant).

SIGURD AND

When Sigurd of the Volsungs was tricked by his teacher Regin into attacking the dragon Fafnir to obtain his hoard of gold, he began an unhappy story that would last for generations.

Sigurd (SEEG uhrd), the son of Sigmund (SEEG muhnd), was the last surviving descendant of the great King Volsung (VOL sung). After Sigmund was killed by King Lyngi of Hunland, Sigurd was adopted by King Alf of Denmark. Everyone loved the boy for his quickness of mind and stoutness of heart. King Alf sent Sigurd to the Dwarf Regin (RAY guhn), who taught Sigurd the arts befitting a prince. But Regin also sowed doubt in Sigurd's mind, "Do you trust your father's family to acknowledge your claim to kingship? Don't they treat you like a stable boy?"

"It is not so!" declared the youth. "But you have no horse, no sword, no wealth of your own," Regin replied. "I can tell you where you can get wealth enough to make you king in your own right."

"Where is this treasure?" asked Sigurd.

"It is guarded by the dragon, Fafnir (FAHF nihr). No king has possessed a greater treasure," replied Regin. "Fafnir is enormous and evil," replied Sigurd. "None dare attack him."

"I believe," said Regin, "that the dragon's reputation far exceeds his actual size and terror. But, if you lack the courage of your ancestors…." "You know I do not!" Sigurd answered angrily. "But what is all this to you? Why do you urge this task?"

Now, Regin, Fafnir, and Otter (OT uhr) were brothers, sons of Hreidmar (HRAYD mahr). Regin had a mind for metals. He could fashion anything from iron, silver, or gold. Otter was a fisher, who could transform himself into the likeness of the creature for which he was named. But Fafnir was darker and stranger and craved gold.

THE DRAGON

Some time earlier, as Otter napped on a river bank, Odin (OH dihn) and Loki (LOH kee) came by. Seeing a well-fed otter, Loki threw a stone and killed it. When the gods realized Otter was Hreidmar's son, they sought Hreidmar out. The old king declared the man price for the killing would be to cover an otter's pelt with gold. This they did, but Loki paid his debt using treasure and a magic ring he stole from the Dwarf Andvari (AHN dwah ree).

The gold whispered to Fafnir day and night. So he killed his father, Hreidmar, and made Andvari's cursed treasure his own. He grew strange and terrible, living alone with his gold. In time, he became a dragon.

"You have lost much!" Sigurd told Regin. "Make me a sword and I will avenge your father!" Regin began work. When the sword was finished, Sigurd smashed it against Regin's anvil to test it, but the sword shattered. "It was not strong enough," Sigurd said.

The same thing happened a second time. So Sigurd went to see his mother, Hjordis (Yor dihs), to get the pieces of his father's shattered sword, Gram, and he brought them to Regin.

"If you forge my father's sword anew, I will be able to destroy Fafnir," Sigurd declared. This time, when the sword was drawn from the forge and tested, it split Regin's anvil in half. "Now, surely, you will avenge me?" Regin asked. "In good time," Sigurd replied. "First, I must first avenge my own father and kin."

So Sigurd went to King Alf and said, "I owe you thanks and reward for your many kindnesses to me, but I must travel to Hunland to face King Lyngi and avenge Sigmund and my kin."

King Alf and his sons loved Sigurd, so they sent him with ships, arms, and men to fulfill his destiny in Hunland. King Lyngi met Sigurd with a great army of his own. Spears filled the air, axes broke helmets, and many warriors fell to the cold earth. Sigurd, his arms covered in blood, waded through the Huns, killing many. When at last, he faced Lyngi, his father's slayer, he brought Gram down on his head, splitting him in half. Sigurd returned to Denmark, his boats loaded with treasure. All hailed him as the greatest of warriors.

Now Regin led Sigurd to the mountain where Fafnir guarded his hoard in a cave. The path worn by the monster between its lair and the lake from which it drank water was enormous. "I thought you said Fafnir's reputation for size and evil was exaggerated?" Sigurd said. "Is the mighty prince frightened by a worm?" sneered Regin. "Dig a hole in the path along which the dragon slithers. When he is above you, stab him."

Alarmed, Sigurd asked, "What will happen when the dragon's venomous blood pours out and fills the hole in which I hide?" Regin stared at Sigurd coldly. "Why bother helping you if you're afraid of everything?"

But as soon as Sigurd began digging, Regin fled. Then Odin, disguised as a beggar with a grey beard, appeared and said to Sigurd, "You labor under bad advice. Dig many pits to catch the dragon's blood, not just one to hide in. This will draw the venomous gore away from you!"

Sigurd did as the beggar advised. Soon Fafnir made his way along the path for a drink. As the beast's belly passed over Sigurd's head, the young warrior saw a gap in the dragon's scales and thrust Gram into the opening. Fafnir thrashed and roared, smashing trees to splinters and casting boulders around like toys.

His life ebbing away, Fafnir finally lay still. He said, "You are Sigurd, son of Sigmund. Regin, my brother, has put you up to this. I tell you, Sigurd, the treasure I guard brings woe to any who possess it. Leave it—and return to your home."

"If leaving your treasure granted immortality, I would ride home at once. But all come to death," replied Sigurd. "Until that final day comes, every brave and true man needs wealth."

Fafnir then breathed his last. What happened to the cursed treasure is another tale.

The World of
SIGURD AND THE DRAGON

Sigurd (SEEG uhrd), a legendary hero of the Norse, appears in the *Volsunga Saga*, written in Iceland in the A.D. 1100's or 1200's. The saga tells of the rise and decline of the Volsung family. It combines Scandinavian folk tales with stories that may be based on real events from the 400's, a period of great change in Europe. During that time, Germanic peoples from central Europe were pushed north into Scandinavia by the expansion of the Roman Empire.

HONOR AND FEUDS

The Germanic peoples of Europe commonly avenged the death of their kin for the honor of the family, as Sigurd avenges his father, Sigmund (SEEG muhnd). Such revenge could lead to feuds between families that were fought for generations, as a man who killed the killer of his kinsman was in turn killed by a member of the other family. The Norse sagas contain details of many such feuds. The killing could be ended only if one or other family paid the other family *wergild* (WUR gihld), or *a man price*, an amount of treasure equal to the value of the slain man.

Sigurd killed the dragon Fafnir (FAHF nihr) using Gram, his father's sword that was shattered and then reforged.

Prince Thorismond (THAWR ihs muhnd) is proclaimed king of the Visigoths after a victorious battle against Attila the Hun and his armies in A.D. 451. The Visigoths were one group of a large confederation of Germanic people called the Goths. The Goths, who helped to destroy the West Roman Empire in the A.D. 400's, probably originated in southern Scandinavia. They migrated to what is now Poland and to the region north of the Black Sea.

Hidden in a pit, the hero Sigurd stabs the dragon Fafnir as he walks to a lake to get a drink of water.

DRAGONS

Dragons appear in myths and folk stories from all around the world. They are usually reptiles with long, serpentlike bodies, small wings, short legs ending in feet equipped with fearsome claws, and a long, scaly tail. From their long, thin heads they can spout fire. In European stories, dragons are traditionally portrayed as ferocious beasts that represent the evils fought by human beings. According to some medieval legends, dragons lived in wild, remote regions of the world. The dragons guarded treasures in their dens, and a person who killed one could gain its wealth. In East Asian mythology, however, dragons are generally considered friendly creatures that ensure good luck and wealth. In China, for example, the dragon is the most powerful of all animals and was used as a symbol of the emperor.

41

THE DEATH OF SIGURD

When Sigurd fell in love with one of Odin's Valkyries—the warrior goddesses who take the dead to Valhalla—their affair was doomed to end in sorrow.

After defeating Fafnir (FAHF nihr), Sigurd (SEEG uhrd) tasted the heart-blood of the dragon. Instantly, he could understand the speech of birds. He entered Fafnir's lair and took a shining war helmet and a ring from the cursed treasure of the Dwarf Andvari (AHN dwah ree). The birds sang, "Heed the dragon's warning, Sigurd. Do not take the whale-road for home. Instead go over land."

Sigurd listened to the birds. Mounting his brave steed, Grani (GRAH nee), Sigurd took mountain roads to Mount Hindfell (HIHND fuhl). There Sigurd saw the House of Flame, a castle with high black walls, ringed by flame. Any other horse and rider would have been terrified, but Sigurd and Grani leaped through the flames and entered the house. Sigurd came to a chamber where a woman in glorious battle gear lay sleeping. Sigurd removed her helmet and breastplate, and the woman woke. "Who disturbs my slumber?" she asked, turning her blue eyes on Sigurd. "I am Sigurd, the son of Sigmund (SEEG muhnd). Who are you, lady?"

"I am Brunhild (BROON hihld), once a Valkyrie (val KIHR ee) in Asgard (AS gahrd)," she said. "I disobeyed Odin (OH dihn), the All-Father, and he cursed me. But before piercing me with the thorn of sleep, Odin predicted that one day the bravest of men would wake me and I would be his wife."

Sigurd told how he had struck down the Huns to avenge his father and later slew Fafnir. "And you passed through the fire-ring!" said Brunhild. "Surely you are the bravest of men." "Perhaps," said Sigurd, "but my heart burns to win greater fame than any warrior before me."

Love came quickly to the Valkyrie and warrior, and for some time Sigurd was lost in Brunhild's deep blue eyes. But hearing Grani neighing in the stable, the young warrior's desire for greatness rekindled. "Release me from your gaze, Brunhild. I must secure my fame and win a kingdom of my own before I can make you my queen," said Sigurd. "Behold, I place this ring on your finger as a pledge of my return."

"Well-spoken, love!" replied Brunhild. "Win fame and endure bravely what it takes to acquire it. I wait, knowing only Sigurd has courage enough to brave the fire-ring and claim me."

Leaving Mount Hindfell, Sigurd rode to the land of the Nibelungs (NEE buh lungs) and the mead hall of King Guiki and Queen Grimhild (GRIHM-hihld). Having heard of Sigurd's strength and courage, the king and queen welcomed him. Soon, Sigurd was an oath-brother of the king's sons, Gunnar (goo nahr) and Hogni. But no oaths bound Sigurd and Guttorm, the king's stepson.

The young men waged war in King Guiki's name. Gunnar and Hogni were valiant, but Sigurd outshone all men in battle and in wisdom. Not content with the oaths already binding Sigurd to the Nibelungs, Queen Grimhild wished him to marry her daughter, Gudrun (GUD roon). The queen, who was a witch, knew that Sigurd's heart belonged to another, so she slipped a potion into Sigurd's drink at a banquet. For days, Sigurd's mind wandered in dreamland. When his mind returned, he had forgotten Brunhild. The next time he saw Gudrun, it was as if for the first time, and they were soon wed.

One day, Sigurd heard the birds say, "How funny! Sigurd does not know the power of the golden helmet he plundered from the dragon's hoard. The helmet bestows a shape-shifter's power on its wearer."

Not long after, Gunnar confessed to Sigurd that he, too, was in love. "With whom?" Sigurd asked. "I do not know her name," Gunnar admitted, "but I have heard that she dwells in a black house surrounded by a ring of fire."

Sigurd laughed at Gunnar. "You are in love with a woman who exists only in stories!?" But, seeing his sincerity, Sigurd added, "Why not? Let us find her."

When they came to Mount Hindfell, Sigurd had no memory of it. The walls of flame frightened Gunnar and his horse, so Sigurd changed shape to look like Gunnar and rode Grani through the fire-ring. That way, it would seem to the woman that Gunnar was saving her.

Brunhild was astonished that another warrior had braved the fire. She challenged the false Gunnar to fight.

Neither could overcome the other until the false Gunnar saw a ring on Brunhild's finger and pulled it off. Without her ring, Brunhild was easily overcome. She agreed to be Gunnar's bride and rode with him on Grani across the fire-ring. Then Sigurd returned to his true shape and rode to the land of the Nibelungs.

When Sigurd saw his wife, Gudrun, he placed Andvari's ring upon her hand and kissed her. Suddenly, he remembered placing the ring on Brunhild's finger and all he had promised her. At that moment, Queen Grimhild's spell was broken. Sigurd's heart was shattered, and again his mind wandered for days. His sadness only deepened when Gunnar and Brunhild returned to the land of the Nibelungs and Gunnar became the king.

Brunhild treated Gudrun, Sigurd's wife, as an inferior, but the Nibelung princess had no idea why. One day, the women quarreled. "As King Gunnar's wife, I rank higher than you," said Brunhild.

"King's wife you may be," said Gudrun, "but my husband is braver than your husband. Sigurd slew Fafnir and claimed the dragon's hoard!" "Perhaps, but Gunnar rode through Odin's fire-ring to win me," replied Brunhild.

"Ha!" said Gudrun, "It was Sigurd in Gunnar's shape who rescued you from the House of Flame. It was he who took from your finger the ring I now wear!" said Gudrun, showing her the ring.

When Brunhild realized that all Gudrun said was true, her shame was deep. She, one of Odin's Valkyries, had been won through falsehood—not by the bravest of men, but by an inferior! Her shame turned to hatred for Sigurd.

Sigurd tried to tell Brunhild that he had been bewitched by Queen Grimhild. He offered Brunhild all of the Dragon Fafnir's treasure hoard as compensation. But Brunhild refused. "It is too late, Sigurd. I have only hate for you!" she cried.

So Brunhild combined serpent's venom and wolf-meat and fed it to Guttorm, Gunnar's stepbrother. The food made Guttorm go mad. At Brunhild's urging, he stabbed Sigurd to death while he slept.

When Sigurd's body was placed aboard his funeral boat, Brunhild lay down next to him and thrust a sword through her own heart. When the Nibelungs set fire to Sigurd's funeral boat, Brunhild once again lay surrounded by flames.

The World of SIGURD AND BRUNHILD

The Germanic peoples of northern Europe—including the Vikings—mixed freely with one another, and many elements of their cultures and myths became mingled. Some Norse myths and stories are closely related to those of other peoples in north and central Europe. The Germanic peoples all spoke forms of early German, but they were not one single group. They included Goths, Vandals, and Huns as well as Angles and Saxons. The Vikings' ancestors included numerous peoples. In Denmark, the Jutes mixed with the Danes, and in Sweden, the Swedes mixed with the Geats and Gutes.

The Valkyries (val KIHR eez) ride to a battlefield to retrieve fallen warriors, in an illustration from the early 1900's. The Valkyries were warlike goddess-maidens who rode horses and were armed with spears, shields, and helmets. At Odin's (OH dihns) command, they led the fallen warriors to Asgard (AS gahrd), the realm of the gods. There, the warriors would live on in a great mead hall dedicated to the glorious dead. The Valkyries could also decide the outcome of a battle and choose who lived and who died. In some stories, Valkyrie could love or even marry a human man.

KENNINGS

When the birds tell Sigurd (SEEG uhrd) not to use the "whale-road"—that is, the sea—for his journey home, they are using a *kenning*, a type of metaphor (MEHT uh fuhr). A metaphor is a figure of speech in which a word or phrase that means one thing is applied to another thing to suggest a likeness between the two. For example, an unsympathetic person may be described metaphorically as having "a heart of stone." Skalds often used kennings. Some other examples include "storm of swords" for "battle" and "wave-traveler" for "boat."

In one version of the myth of Sigurd, Gudrun (GUD roon) (seated) marries King Atli (AHT lee) (left), a character loosely based on Attila (AT uh luh), the notorious leader of the Huns, after Sigurd is murdered. In revenge for Atli's murder of her family, however, Gudrun kills her two sons by the king and serves them to him at a feast. After he finishes his meal, she tells him what she has done and then kills Atli and all his men by setting fire to their mead hall.

Brunhild (BROON hihld) is punished by Odin because she failed to obey his will when judging a fight between two kings. Although she knew that Odin preferred one of the kings, Brunhild named the other king as victor.

VAINAMOINEN
and the Creation of the World

The Finns told this story to explain how the world was created and how farming was first introduced to their forested homelands.

In the beginning, there was Ukko (OO goh), the Sky God, and the boundless waters. Ilmatar (EEL mah tahr), Ukko's daughter and the goddess of air, floated in endless space but wished for something more. She floated to the First Sea and settled upon it. For hundreds of years, fierce winds buffeted her and waves tossed her. Although she wished to return to her former home, she could not. "Woe is me!" cried Ilmatar. "Why did I leave the gentle sky for this rough and watery world? Every movement is pain as I wander this endless ocean. Ukko, Father, help me!"

Almost at once, a beautiful duck swept down from the sky, but it found nowhere to land. Ilmatar raised her knees as a

place for the duck to build her nest. The duck took shelter and laid seven eggs— six of gold and one of iron.

As the duck warmed the eggs with her body, Ilmatar's knees began to burn. Ilmatar flinched, and the eggs tumbled from their nest into the water. The eggs broke open, and their pieces were transformed into wondrous things. The bottom half of one shell became Earth. The top half became the arch of heaven. The yolks became sunlight; the whites became moonbeams. Some pieces became stars, and others, clouds.

And so the visible world was made, and ages rolled by as the sun rose and set, the moon and stars following

Ilmatar now floated in Earth's ocean. In time, she desired to create beautiful things. She lifted up lands, separating them from the sea. She created the depths for fish and planted the reefs and islands. Then she rested.

Now, during all this time, Ilmatar carried Vainamoinen (VY nuh moy nehn), a child of the wind, within her. But after hundreds of years, Vainamoinen grew restless within Ilmatar. The sun, moon, and stars of the Great Bear heard his cries but would not help him escape. At last, Vainamoinen burst forth into the ocean. For eight years, he swam about, growing familiar with the world around him. He then hauled himself ashore and stood up.

For some time, Vainamoinen considered who should sow the barren Earth. He appointed the god Sampsa Pellervoinen (pehl ehr voy nehn), the Wise and Ancient One, to plant seeds. Sampsa Pellervoinen sowed trees and plants of every description, and pines, junipers, linden, birch, and alders sprang up.

As Vainamoinen surveyed the forests, he noticed that the oak tree had not sprouted, and wondered why this should be. Then in the distance, he saw five water-sprites on a finger of land. They were raking grass into long rows.

After they were finished, Tursas (tur sahs), a sea-giant, rose from the water and pushed down on the grass-rows, which then started to burn. When the grass had been reduced to ash, Tursas spread the ash and placed an acorn in its midst. The acorn sprouted and soon a mighty oak reached the skies, capturing the clouds in its branches and blocking out sunlight. "This is not good! Gods and people need sunlight," Vainamoinen cried out. "Mother Ilmatar, lend me water forces to chop down this evil oak!"

A small figure sprang from the sea, no larger than a man's forefinger. He looked like a tiny warrior; his clothing was green and trimmed with copper. "Are you a god or a mortal, little one?" asked Vainamoinen. "I am a god, a hero of the sea deities. I have come to chop down the oak," replied the tiny being. "What can one so small do against the mighty oak?" scoffed Vainamoinen.

Instantly, the tiny copper-and-green man grew into a huge giant with hair flowing to his ankles and a beard reaching to his knees. With blows of his axe, the giant felled the tree with a crash that shook heaven and Earth.

Branches, leaves, trunk, and bark scattered in all directions. The splinters of the great oak floated atop the blue-black sea to the Northland. The land's guardian spirit used the splinters to make magical arrows for Vainamoinen.

Everything that Sampsa Pellervoinen had planted was now growing, except the barley. While Vainamoinen tried to figure out why this was so, a titmouse called, "Barley will not flourish unless the soil is made ready."

Sampsa Pellervoinen, the Wise and Ancient One, understood. He fashioned an ax and cleared the forest, leaving only the birches standing to give the sacred birds and eagles a home. The other trees he burnt to cinders, working ashes into the soil. Once all was prepared, Vainamoinen sowed barley seeds, praying as he worked.

Father Ukko heard this prayer and sent rain upon the freshly planted field. Eight days later, Vainamoinen saw the first shoots pushing forth from the soil. The leaves were triple-knotted, and the ears of barley were six-sided. Vainamoinen looked about him and was very pleased with what he had achieved.

The World of
VAINAMOINEN

The ancestors of the Finns arrived in what is now Finland more than 5,000 years ago. Their original homeland may have been between the Volga River and the Ural Mountains in what is now Russia. At that time, the ancestors of the Sami (SAH mee), the native people of Finland, lived farther inland and more to the north. At first, the Finns lived as *nomadic* (traveling) hunters and gatherers. They eventually adopted farming and the raising of animals. The Finns gradually pushed the Sami—who continued to rely on hunting, gathering, and fishing—farther and farther north. The early Finns were divided into three loosely organized tribes that often fought one another.

The central character in the *Kalevala* (kah luh vah luh), Finland's national epic story, is Vainamoinen (VY nuh moy nehn), a god who possesses magical powers. Vainamoinen is the creator of the Finns; a shaman, who links humans to the supernatural world; a magician; and a famous *bard* (poet). At the end of the *Kalevala*, Vainamoinen is driven into exile by Finland's first Christian king. This echoes the process by which the traditional religion of the Finns was replaced by Christianity and shows how elements of Finnish history—some of it prehistoric—are woven into the epic's mythological elements.

The Great Bear (right) is a constellation also known as Ursa Major. The Great Bear includes a group of seven stars known as the Big Dipper. The cup of the Big Dipper forms the back of the bear, the handle forms the tail, and fainter stars outline the head and legs. An imaginary line that extends from the two stars at the front of the cup points to Polaris (poh LAIR ihs), the North Star. Polaris appears stationary, while other stars seem to revolve as Earth rotates. As a result, Polaris has served as a guide for navigators through the centuries.

A NATIONAL EPIC

Many of the Finns' ancient storytelling traditions still existed when Elias Lonrott, a country doctor, began collecting Finnish oral, or spoken, folklore and myth in the 1820's. Lonrott's huge collection, called the *Kalevala* (Land of Kavela), became Finland's national epic. The *Kalevala* begins with a creation story and is filled with stories of battle, the search for magical powers, romance, destruction and reconstruction. The epic ends with the coming of Christianity to Finland.

Traditional Finnish clothing included brightly colored clothes and caps.

ILMARINEN
Creates the Sampo

To the Finns, this story described the origins of a mythical magical object of enormous value, the Sampo, which features in a number of stories in the *Kalevala*.

Vainamoinen (VY nuh moy nehn), master of magic, had an archenemy. This young man, who was named Joukahainen (YO kuh hy nehn), had challenged Vainamoinen to a singing contest. But Vainamoinen had triumphed with his glorious voice and powerful songs. Enraged, Joukahainen struck down Vainamoinen in a surprise attack.

For many weary days, Vainamoinen floated on the blue-black seas, powerless, drifting with the waves. One day, a swift eagle swooped down and carried Vainamoinen to Pohjola (POH yoh lah), the never-pleasant Northland. Louhi (LOH hee), the queen of Pohjola, held Vainamoinen captive, subjecting him to many torments.

"You will never leave the Northland, Vainamoinen. You will never again see the beautiful plains of Vainola, never breathe the sweet air of Kaleva (kah-luh-vah)," said the cruel queen. "If you release me, I will make you the Sampo," Vainamoinen said. "I promise to send Ilmarinen (EEL mah ree nuhn), the master smith, to make you this all-powerful charm."

Queen Louhi agreed to the bargain and released Vainamoinen, who returned to Kaleva. On the Osmo Plain, he sang into existence a tall fir tree. Vainamoinen then returned to his home. Entering Ilmarinen's smithy, Vainamoinen found the smith working with his hammer by the forge.

"Vainamoinen!" exclaimed Ilmarinen, "Where have you been?" "I've been a prisoner in Pohjola, the Northland, held by people skilled in witchcraft,"

Vainamoinen replied. "I have much to tell. Among the people of Pohjola is a maiden of magical beauty. She will be yours if you go to her land and make the Sampo for Queen Louhi."

"You have promised me to the Northlanders to ransom your own head, crafty Vainamoinen," said Ilmarinen. "I will never go to dismal Pohjola, not for all the beautiful maidens in that land!"

"Let me then show you a wonder on the Osmo Plain," said Vainamoinen. "It is a majestic fir I have conjured. The moon gleams in its needles; the stars of the Great Bear shine on its crown."

"This I doubt, brother," said Ilmarinen, but when they arrived on the plain, the master of metals was filled with wonder at the fir. It was just as Vainamoinen had said. "Climb this tree, Ilmarinen," said Vainamoinen, "gather from its branches moonbeams and the light of the Great Bear. Great power they will give to your metal working."

Ilmarinen climbed eagerly to the top of the tree. But tricky Vainamoinen sang down the storm winds. These winds bore Ilmarinen to the dismal realm of Queen Louhi.

Queen Louhi invited Ilmarinen into her house and laid before him a splendid feast. Her daughter, beautiful beyond description, joined them.

"Tell me, smith," said the queen, "Can you really forge the Sampo? Can you fashion its lid of many colors from swan feathers, the milk of virtue, a single grain of barley, and the finest lambs wool?" "Need you ask?" Ilmarinen replied, "I forged the arch of heaven, a container for the air. I can also make the Sampo, fashioning its lid of many colors." "Then you shall have my daughter as wife," said the queen.

On the three days of Midsummer, Ilmarinen mixed metals in a cauldron and placed the cauldron in the forge. Servants worked the forge's bellows and fed its fire without stopping.

On the first day, Ilmarinen peered in the cauldron and saw a mighty bow. But the bow was evil, asking for the blood of two heroes daily. So the smith broke up the bow and returned it to the cauldron. On the second day, a purple ship appeared in the cauldron. But it, too, was evil, demanding conflict without a cause. So Ilmarinen broke the boat into pieces and returned it to the cauldron. On the third day, a heifer appeared. She was also evil, running wild and wasting her milk. The smith cut the heifer in pieces and threw them into the cauldron.

The fourth day proved no better, as an evil plow arose from the cauldron. The plow would destroy fields and crops. So Ilmarinen chased away the servants who had been working in his smithy. He let the storm winds work as bellows, heating the flames beneath the cauldron. A mighty flame arose, sending smoke and sparks into the sky.

The Sampo with its lid of many colors appeared within the cauldron. Ilmarinen snatched it with his tongs, working it with his hammer. When finished, the Sampo moved back and forth, grinding grain—some for eating, some for market, some for the storehouse. Queen Louhi was delighted.

Ilmarinen approached the beautiful maiden. "I have forged the Sampo. Will you accompany me to Kaleva to live as my wife?" But Queen Louhi's daughter refused. So the queen sent Ilmarinen home in a copper boat. Heavy-hearted, Ilmarinen returned to the blessed land of Kaleva, singing, "I made the mighty Sampo for the queen of the dismal North. She has her treasure, but I have not the beautiful maiden."

The World of ILMARINEN

Ilmarinen (EEL mah ree nuhn) is one of the many magical *smiths* (metalworkers) who appear in world myths. They include Vulcan (VUHL kuhn) in Roman mythology; Hephaestus (hih FEHS tuhs) in Greek mythology; Goibhniu (GOY nee oo) in Celtic mythology; and Ogun (OH guhn) in the mythology of the Yoruba (YOH ru bah) in what is now Nigeria. Smiths are often credited with possessing great and mysterious power. This may reflect their ability to transform rock into metal by heating it in fire, which is a process also commonly used in magical transformations. The power of smiths also reflects the importance of iron in human history. Learning to use iron to make tools for farming and weapons for fighting was a major technological achievement.

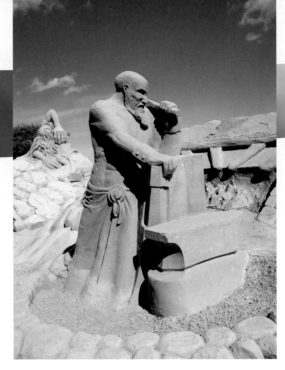

A figure of Ilmarinen was sculpted from sand for a festival in Finland in 2013.

A Sami (SAH mee) family camps in northern Finland. The Sami were formerly known as Lapps, but they prefer the name Sami. Experts estimate that there are between 70,000 and 100,000 Sami. A few thousand live in Finland and Russia. Most live in Norway and Sweden. The governments and the other peoples in the countries where the Sami live sometimes regarded Sami customs as backward and pagan. Such attitudes began to change in the mid-1900's. Traditional Sami clothing and the traditional song form, the joik, have become sources of Sami pride. Many people admire the traditional Sami respect for land and the environment. Some Sami still travel with reindeer as the herds migrate between summer pastures and winter pastures. But most Sami live in towns and villages. Some live and work in cities.

WHAT WAS THE SAMPO?

Scholars disagree on what sort of object the Sampo was. Some suggest that it was a kind of compass or perhaps a treasure chest. This story suggests that it was a *mill* (grinding machine) that could produce grain from nothing, thus becoming a source of great wealth. Later in the *Kalevala* (kah luh vah luh), Ilmarinen and Vainamoinen (VY nuh moy nehn) steal the Sampo from Louhi's (LOH heez) fortress because Louhi refused to give Ilmarinen her beautiful daughter in exchange for his labor.

Ilmarinen, the hero-smith, forges the Sampo in his smithy. The objects that appear in Ilmarinen's cauldron were central to life for the Finns in their traditional lifestyle. The bow reflected the importance of warfare in early Scandinavia, when the Finns displaced the Sami from their territory. The boat reflects traditions of both fishing and trading overseas.

The plow that appears in the cauldron is a symbol of wheat and other crops.

The heifer in the cauldron is a reminder of the importance of dairy farms to life in Finland.

DEITIES OF SCANDINAVIA

Aesir (EYE seer)
The Aesir were a family of warrior gods that included Odin, Thor, and Loki who lived in Asgard.

Angrboda (AHNG guhr boh duh)
A giantess, Angrboda had three monstrous children with Loki, the Trickster god: Jormungandr, Hel, and Fenrir.

Balder (BAWL duhr)
"The Shining One," Balder was the god of light and beauty who was much loved by the other gods. Because of Loki, he died and was forced to remain in the underworld, despite the gods' efforts to free him.

Bestla (BEHST lah)
One of Ymir's daughters. Bestla gave birth to three sons, Odin, Vili, and Vé, who founded the first race of gods.

Bor (bawr)
The son of the giant Buri, Bor became the husband of Bestla and the father of Odin, Vili, and Vé.

Brunhild (BROON hihld)
Brunhild was originally a Valkyrie, but after she disobeyed Odin, she was imprisoned on a mountain in a magic ring of fire, until she was rescued by Sigurd.

Buri (BOO ree)
The first Norse god, who came into being as he was licked out of the ice by the first cow; Buri created Bor and founded the Norse pantheon of gods.

Fafnir (FAHF nihr)
The son of a king, Fafnir transformed into a dragon because of his lust for gold.

Fenrir (fehn rihr)
A monstrous wolf, Fenrir was the son of Loki the Trickster and the giantess Angrboda. He was destined to kill Odin at Ragnarok.

Freyja (FRAY uh)
Goddess of love and fertility, Freyja was also queen of the Valkyries, going into battle on a chariot drawn by two cats.

Freyr (frayr)
Twin brother of Freyja and son of Njord (the Norse sea god), Freyr was the god of peace and prosperity.

Frigg (frihg)
Married to Odin and mother to Balder, she managed to protect her son from everything harmful in the world except mistletoe.

Hel
Goddess of the dead, Hel ruled the cold, dank region of Helheim (the Norse underworld) and was hideously ugly.

Hermod (HER mood),
Hermod, Balder's brother, went to hell to plead for Balder's life and was rewarded for his loyalty by being made the host of Valhalla.

Idun (EE duhn)
Idun was the keeper of the golden Apples of Eternal Youth, which the gods ate to stay young.

Ilmarinen (EEL mah ree nuhn)
The mythical Finnish master *smith* (metalworker) was the creator of the Sampo.

Ilmatar (EEL mah tahr)
Goddess of air in Finnish folklore, she was the mother of Vainamoinen, with whom she was pregnant for 730 years.

Jormungandr (YAWR muhn guhn dahr)
A serpent, Jormungandr grew to surround Midgard, the home of humans. He was fated to kill Thor during Ragnarok (the battle that ends the world).

Loki (LOH kee)
The Norse trickster god, Loki, was famously malicious in his dealings with other gods, and was made to suffer punishment until Ragnarok began.

Mimir (MEE mihr)
Mimir was the talking head at the bottom of the Tree of Wisdom. He was frequently consulted by the gods.

Njord (nyoord)
The Norse god of the sea, Njord had power over the waves, fire, and the wind.

Norns
The three Norn goddesses (Urd, Verdandi, and Skuld) were in charge of the threads of fate, which they wove and tied to decide humans' destinies.

Odin (OH dihn)
The all-powerful Norse father of the gods, Odin was one of the most complex gods of any civilization. Odin looks after war, death, and knowledge.

Sampsa Pellervoinen (pehl ehr voy nehn)
The Wise and Ancient One, Pellervoinen was sometimes Vainamoinen's brother in Finnish mythology. He was the god of crops and nature.

Sigyn (SEHG ihn)
Loki's wife, she was famous for her patience. She devoted her time to trying to lessen the torments he suffered as punishment.

Skadi (SKAW dee)
Skadi, also known as "the Devourer," was the Norse goddess of the hunt.

Thor (thawr)
Muscular Norse thunder-god, Thor had a hammer (Mjollnir) that he used to create lightning. The rumbling of his chariot wheels created the thunder.

Tyr (tihr)
Tyr was Odin's trusted companion and dispenser of justice in battle.

Ukko (OO goh)
The Finnish Sky Father, Ukko was the husband to the Earth mother goddess, Akka.

Vainamoinen (VY nuh moy nehn)
Ilmatar's son, Vainamoinen was a popular hero-god, who featured in many Finnish myths.

Valkyrie (val KIHR ee)
A warlike goddess-maiden who rode a swift horse. Odin, the chief god, sent the Valkyries to battlefields to retrieve fallen heroes and lead them to Asgard.

Vanir (VAH nihr)
The Vanir were nature gods and rivals of the Aesir.

Ymir (EE mihr)
The first living thing on Earth, Ymir was a Frost Giant who is killed by his grandson Odin.

GLOSSARY

alliteration Repeating the same letter or sound at the start of words that are next to one another.

blood brothers Men who have sworn to treat each other as brothers, usually with a ceremony in which they mix their blood.

Edda A collection of old Norse stories or poems.

epic A long traditional poem reciting the deeds of legendary heroes from the history of a nation.

feud A long and bitter dispute between two families that is often carried down over a series of generations.

forge To make an object by heating metal and hitting or shaping it. A forge is also the place where this happens.

gore Blood that has been shed as a result of violence.

immortality The quality of being able to live forever.

kenning A figure of speech in which two words are put together to create a metaphorical definition of a third thing.

longhouse A long dwelling in which a Viking family lived, with space for their animals in winter.

man-price (wergild) A monetary value set on a man's life which must be paid to his family by his killer.

mead An alcoholic drink made by fermenting honey with yeast.

mead hall A long hall for feasting and entertainment.

moral Concerned with the principles of right and wrong behavior.

myth A traditional story that a people tell to explain their own origins or the origins of natural and social phenomena. Myths often involve gods, spirits, and other supernatural beings.

oath A solemn promise about one's future actions or behavior.

pantheon A collection of all the gods and goddesses of a religion.

prophetess A woman who has the ability to foretell the future.

ransom A payment made for the safe return of someone or something that has been taken away.

ritual A solemn religious ceremony in which a set of actions are performed in a specific order.

sacred Something that is connected with the gods or goddesses and so should be treated with respectful worship.

saga A long Norse story about a heroic achievement.

skald A composer who creates and recites poems about the deeds of heroes.

supernatural Describes something that cannot be explained by science or by the laws of nature, which is therefore said to be caused by beings such as gods, spirits, or ghosts.

warlord A chieftain who can command a group of warriors.

FOR FURTHER INFORMATION

Books

Allan, Tony. *Exploring the Life, Myth, and Art of the Vikings* (Civilizations of the World). Rosen Publishing Group, 2012.

Daly, Kathleen N. *Norse Mythology A to Z (Mythology A to Z)*. Chelsea House Publishers, 2010.

D'Aulaire, Ingrid, and Edgar Parin D'Aulaire. *D'Aulaire's Book of Norse Myths*. (New York Review Children's Collection) New York Review of Books, 2005.

Davis, Graeme. *Thor: Viking God of Thunder* (Myths and Legends). Osprey Publishing, 2013.

Hoena, Blake. *Everything Mythology (National Geographic Kids: Everything series)*. National Geographic Society, 2014.

Hopkins, Adrea. *Viking Gods and Legends* (The Viking Library). Powerkids Press, 2002.

Husain, Shahrukh. *Vikings* (Stories from Ancient Civilizations). SmartApple Media, 2005.

Long, Steven. *Odin: The Viking Allfather* (Myths and Legends). Osprey Publishing, 2015.

Makinen, Kirsti. *The Kalevala: Tales of Magic and Adventure*. Simply Read Books, 2009.

Nardo, Don. *The Vikings* (World History). Lucent Books, 2010.

National Geographic Essential Visual History of World Mythology. National Geographic Society, 2008.

Philip, Neil. *Eyewitness Mythology* (DK Eyewitness Books). DK Publishing, 2011.

Redmond, Shirley-Raye. *Norse Mythology (Mythology and Culture Worldwide)*. Lucent Books, 2012.

Schomp, Virginia. *The Vikings* (People of the Ancient World). Franklin Watts, 2005.

Weintraub, Aileen. *Vikings: Raiders and Explorers* (Way of the Warrior). Children's Press, 2005.

Williams, Brian. *Understanding Norse Myths* (Myths Understood). Crabtree Publishing Company, 2013.

Websites

http://www.godchecker.com/pantheon/norse-mythology.php
A directory of Norse deities from God Checker, written in a light-hearted style but with accurate information.

http://www.pantheon.org/areas/mythology/europe/norse/
Encyclopedia Mythica page with links to many pages about Norse myths. Click on the link to "available articles."

http://www.mythome.org/nordic.html
A page with links to articles about the different Norse gods.

http://www.crystalinks.com/vikings.html
This Crystal Links page has links to pages about all aspects of Viking culture, including its gods, goddesses, and myths.

http://www.bbc.co.uk/schools/primaryhistory/vikings/beliefs_and_stories/
A BBC website about the Vikings that includes a collection of animated Viking stories, interactive quizzes, and printable activities.

INDEX

PRONUNCIATION KEY

Sound	As in
a	hat, map
ah	father, far
ai	care, air
aw	order
aw	all
ay	age, face
ch	child, much
ee	equal, see
ee	machine, city
eh	let, best
ih	it, pin, hymn
k	coat, look
o	hot, rock
oh	open, go
oh	grow, tableau
oo	rule, move, food
ow	house, out
oy	oil, voice
s	say, nice
sh	she, abolition
u	full, put
u	wood
uh	cup, butter
uh	flood
uh	about, ameba
uh	taken, purple
uh	pencil
uh	lemon
uh	circus
uh	labyrinth
uh	curtain
uh	Egyptian
uh	section
uh	fabulous
ur	term, learn, sir, work
y	icon, ice, five
yoo	music
zh	pleasure